Collapsing Democracies

The battle for power and survival

CHRIS SHEPPARD

ISBN: 9798374602920

CONTENTS

AUTHOR

Chris Sheppard C.Eng, FIMechE, BSc

Now retired, my early career experience was in British Rail Workshops Division, and later as Executive Director before privatisation. As Managing Director of Customer Support, I was responsible for the successful restructuring and decentralisation of the Customer Support side of the Company, becoming a world leader in this "after market" activity, with operations across all continents. This specialism involved transforming the performance of acquired state owned workshops and depots, whilst also changing the focus of the Company from a simple supplier of new vehicles at lowest price to a supplier including long term maintenance and performance guarantees, with change of design focus to include reliability and maintainability. The Company, BREL, was acquired by ABB, became ADTRANZ, before becoming Daimler Chrysler Rail Division, when I was President of the Customer Support Division before retirement.

PREFACE

Public anger at the increasingly poor quality of public services in democracies is becoming a threat to democracy itself. Either Governments and their State Sectors are oblivious to this, or have no idea as to the cause or solution.

Incredibly, two in-laws, myself and Marcos Barros, who specialise in overcoming the "Chains of Bureaucracy" in their differing fields, came together through their children and are the prime activists in helping Brazil, one of the largest Democracies in the World, to transform the performance of its Public Services. After an initial conference and contract to improve the performance of the public sector, their second major conference presentation, this time to 700 State Sector senior managers, was also in the State of Mato Grosso Do Sul in October 2022. Marcos Barros, an International Management Consultant from Shrewsbury, specialising in the application of OKRs (Objectives and Key Results), is now spreading the recent rapid improvement in services to other States such as the Federal District, where Brasilia is also the country's capital. We have been invited to lead an even larger conference in 2023, to encourage the spread of improvements across the whole of Brazil. I am a "support act", now in retirement, but sharing my own Public Sector and Private Sector international experiences in overcoming bureaucracy. This improved the performance of rail repair workshops, creating a private sector world leader in the repair and service sector of Railways. Both a

30% efficiency improvement and vastly improved customer satisfaction were consistently achieved within 1 year, helping to transform the performance of the operating railways in the 90s, a decade when passenger traffic in the UK doubled over 10 years, with passenger satisfaction being one of the highest in Europe.

Various academic papers, referred to in Chapter 3, show a significant rise in public dissatisfaction with the quality of governance in democracies. This is resulting in an increase in populism of left and right, with a decline in democratic freedoms across ten countries over the 15 years to 2018, after continuous democratisation growth over the previous 200 years. The growth curve has moved beyond the dangerous point of inflection, which suggests that the move back to autocracies could accelerate, unless urgent corrective action is taken. Recent events confirm this danger.

The purpose of this book is to analyse the cause of this disillusionment and the common bureaucratic governance "flaws" across nearly all democracies. It offers proven solutions to enable democracies to rapidly restore their credibility and resist a new generation of autocrats. The specific details of how to apply this are contained in the "sister" book "Breaking The Chains Of Bureaucracy" (Amazon), which I co-authored with Marcos Barros and also details the rapidly spreading governance successes in Brazil, which is being inspired by Marcos with their enthusiastic Leaders.

Without corrective action, bureaucracies will inevitably destroy the credibility of many more Public Services and Democracies over the next 10 years.

1 - INTRODUCTION

This book focuses on the threats and evolving role of organisation structures on the governance of both democracies and autocracies. However, it is also necessary to understand the historical driving forces and time frames, the fragility of democracies and the impact of education and rapidly changing technologies on all aspects of governance. This should evolve to enable public expectations to be met. It is also relevant to understand the reasons for the devolved organisation structures of successful private companies over the last 40 years. The contrast between the performance of these dynamic and customer focused companies and the introverted, cumbersome public services is increasing and clear for all to see.

Historical evolvement

The World has seen the rise and fall of many autocratic Empires, which were prerequisites for both conflict and survival. They have contributed in a variety of ways to the cultures of today. Following the Roman Conquests, slavery was expanded and "industrialised". The early steps towards democratisation encouraged the evolvement of the British Empire, Europe and USA away from slavery. In Britain, during the late 18th century, the Monarchy ceded power to Parliament. and the Royal Navy established the West African Squadron in 1808 to suppress the Atlantic slave trade, capturing 1,600 slave ships and freeing 150,000 slaves. The UK Slavery Abolition Act of 1833 abolished the institution of slavery. Significantly, private enterprises in the early tentative democracies were taking the initiative to create new industries and the industrial revolution began. However, the lack of education and slowly evolving technologies resulted in strict central controls being needed to ensure quality and safety standards. Autocracies initially resisted industrialisation on the basis that they could lose control to organised labour in the new industries. Stricter central control was the "solution".

The fight for democracy has been a hard battle across most of the world over the last four centuries with significant evolvement as follows;

a. The 18/19th centuries saw slow progress, with only 10% of countries being considered as democratised.

b. The early 20th century, after the First World War, saw a significant increase.

c. The end of the Second World War saw a further escalation to democracy as countries realised that the scale of threat from narcissistic dictators with atomic bombs was potentially catastrophic.

d. A third significant increase occurred in the late 20th Century, with the collapse of the Soviet Empire. Around 65% (127) of all countries had then been democratised. The major exceptions to this trend were Russia, China and the Middle East, including their satellite countries, plus some Latin American, African and Asian countries. Their "driving forces" were a mixture of Communism, oil, religion and poverty, which encouraged autocrats.

The immaturity and fragility of European democracy is best illustrated by the fact that Hitler came to power through the democratic process, driven by Germany's serious post World War One economic problems. Hitler then took control of most of Europe. The united strength of the British Empire and its armed forces were fundamental to defeating Hitler and Japan, combined, of course, with the later critical involvement of the USA and Russia in 1941. This followed the Japanese attack on Pearl Harbour, coupled with the declaration of war on the USA and Russia by the new German Empire and Italy. Global Democracy itself was under threat. Post war, votes for women were only permitted in Switzerland in the 1960s, when some Southern European countries were also finally democratised.

Today, democratic "Empires" no longer exist, but have been replaced by NATO, a democratic defence organisation committed to the defence of any member subject to attack.

Whilst not wanting to dwell on analysing the reasons for the fall of Empires generally, the prime reasons for the fall of the Roman Empire are generally accepted as being economic, reduction in military capability and poor quality of governance across a huge area. This is relevant when comparing the threats to current democracies.

Post World War Two

After World War Two, the veneer of a more civilised behaviour with the creation of the United Nations and international trading, legal and banking frameworks, for example, were thought to have brought in an era of dialogue and collaboration between both democracies and autocracies worldwide. A new generation of democracies blossomed across Europe and the World, including the countries in the former British Empire, who adopted democracy and voluntarily became members of the "Commonwealth of Countries". Additionally, the collapse of the USSR in 1989 also brought an end to the previous "Cold War", bringing an era of optimism and democracy across Eastern Europe, with the hope that Russia would ultimately follow. This post war period released the energies of private enterprise and a dynamic capitalist sector, continually striving for innovation and growth. Creating and satisfying public demands were core to success, together with a rule of law and agreed international legal frameworks. As education standards improved and the rate of change of technologies and services increased rapidly, particularly towards the end of the century, so the centralised, functional management structures of large private companies became incapable of responding to changing public demand and also the more dynamic and rapidly growing numbers of localised and competitive smaller companies. This resulted in creation of customer focused, decentralised management structures in the private sector in the 80s, epitomised by the world leading international engineering company ABB. I was a senior Executive in this Company, reporting to Perci Barnavic, the President, and was responsible for growing the business of maintenance, repair and refurbishment of rail vehicles across all continents. This started with the initial privatisation of 4 BREL workshops. Before retirement I was President of this Division under Daimler Chrysler ownership, with order intake having increased by a factor of 10 over the previous 10 years. The concept of new vehicles being supported by 10 year maintenance contracts was also introduced, resulting in suppliers focusing on life cycle maintenance costs and reliability, rather than low purchase price with consequences.

Post war, the economies of major democracies have grown, along with quality of life, education, health and social care improvements, coupled with major technology advancements, particularly since 1980. Participation of autocracies was encouraged into this "global market", in the belief that the size of market would grow and democracy would become irresistible. However, if autocratic leaders and their core "team" can become incredibly wealthy from this "openness", with also the general population benefitting to some degree, why would they relinquish their power? There has been a failure to recognise the reality that power, greed and selfishness are fundamental human characteristics that need to be controlled, even in our rapidly evolving attempts at creating a civilised world. Germany is now learning this reality, after their naive trust in Putin to not exploit their evolving total dependence on Russian energy supplies. Are they doing the same with their growing involvement with China? Incredibly, extreme right wing armed activists have recently tried to take control of their Government and demonstrators have stormed Government buildings in the USA and Brazil.

The Peak of Democratisation

The attempt at democracy and privatisation in Russia was badly managed after the collapse of the USSR in the late 80s, which allowed a group of oligarchs, criminal gangs and drug barons to rapidly take control of major sectors of the economy, resulting in economic collapse and a new protected autocracy being formed later under Putin. Surely a salutary lesson for all democracies, that internal security and law and order are fundamental to good governance. The 21st century also started badly with the Islamic terrorist attack on New York, followed by a retaliatory attack on Iraq. State sponsored Islamist terrorism was growing, with conflict between various Middle Eastern autocracies, who are also a major source of oil for the West. Realignment of these autocracies could present real risks for democracies. The alarm bells should have been ringing loud and clear. Since the emergence of Putin followed by the 2007 banking crisis, Russia has moved to an expansionist strategy, with Putin's annexation of Crimea, involvement in conflicts in the Middle East, followed by his attack on Ukraine, which was also coupled with other general expansionist declarations and nuclear threats. In addition to this, the recent COVID pandemic has also caused a significant impact on global economies, with cumbersome bureaucracy also handicapping rapid response.

The steadily increasing power and influence of the Chinese autocracy across the world is also presenting a current and future threat to democracies, which is exemplified by the annexing of Hong Kong, in contravention of an International Agreement, plus its threat to annexe Taiwan, which would give China control of the majority of the global "micro chip" market. With China taking shareholding in many key global industries, whilst also placing legal obligation on those involved to report back to China on "matters of importance" to the Chinese State, the potential threat to Democracies is increasing. China has benefitted enormously by being encouraged to participate in the global market, with the West closing its eyes to human rights and Intellectual Property violations. The attraction of this huge new market has become a spiders web of entrapment, leaving democracies dependent on their low cost key components and their increasing investments in global core activities and resources. When comparing the antagonism of the EU towards the UK for leaving the EU and also to its inaction over the Chinese annexation of Hong Kong and token gesturing over Russia's annexation of Crimea, then it can be seen that

Western Democracies are losing focus on their core governance and security responsibilities and are giving encouragement to autocrats like Putin and Xi to take advantage. It is therefore understandable that the public globally is also unconcerned and may take self indulgent actions which inadvertently accelerate the collapse of democracies themselves. In the UK in particular, in contrast to other countries, the continual attempt by the media and activists to undermine self esteem for being British is doing the work of our enemies. Other countries are careful not to do this, fostering National pride, but self deprecation is a British characteristic which could ultimately undermine us.

Increasing Vulnerability of Democracies

When considering one of the prime responsibilities of governance is security, the fact that the EU is currently supporting NATO with only around 1% of GDP, 50% of the agreed 2%, then it can be seen that over 10 years, the extent of underinvestment in the military by the EU is equivalent to 10% of the EU GDP, around 1.7 trillion US dollars at today's values. With poor management resulting in only 50% of military equipment available for use in Germany, for example, if this is applied across all EU countries, then of the 1.7 trillion USD actually spent over 10 years, only 0.85 trillion USD is available for use, compared to what should have been 3.4 trillion USD total expenditure. This has been a catastrophic neglect of support to NATO, which is the prime defender of democracies and could well undermine the ability to give ongoing support to Ukraine, or even EU NATO members subjected to new attacks. When considering the consistent expansionist threats made by Putin, China, North Korea and Iran over the last 20 years, this response represents a failure of a prime role of governance. It also demonstrates a fragmentation of support for NATO, with France now advocating an independent EU military force, no doubt giving further encouragement to Russia and China. With Trump possibly returning as leader of the USA, will he carry out his threat to withdraw support for Europe if they continue to not contribute the agreed 2% of GDP? There must be a strong case for saying that those countries which have not paid their agreed levy should pay recompense to those who have given a disproportionate amount of support to Ukraine, which has halted Putin's declared aim of wider control of neighbouring countries, including EU countries. The EU claim that they are unable to afford the 2%, unlike the USA, UK and France? How can they afford an EU army?

The responsiveness of all democracies to these challenges over the last 20 years has been questionable at best, As a consequence, Authoritarians and Dictatorships such as Russia, China, North Korea and Iran see that Western Democracies are becoming increasingly weak in terms of Governance, whilst also being self indulgent and economically self sacrificing concerning pollution control, encouraging them to seize any opportunity to extend their power base. Their short term economic advantage is enhanced if they themselves do not comply with UN Human Rights and Trade Laws, or International Intellectual Property and Climate Change Agreements and associated costs. They suffer no penalties, with the West continuing to trade with them, consequently putting their own industries and countries at a huge economic disadvantage.

By ensnaring gullible democracies into dependence on their low cost products, polluting energy sources and loans with penal default terms, they have also taken over the latest technologies developed by the West with no transitional vulnerability or cost to themselves. The West has allowed themselves to become economically dependant on high tech core products and rare materials from authoritarian states, a potential disaster waiting to happen. Even in 2022, a German car company is sourcing assembly away from the West to China. As a "thank you", China has announced that it is now to increase its investment into military equipment in response to perceived "threats from the West"! It almost seems that China is testing how far it can humiliate EU countries in order to test their economic resilience or desperation before embarking on its own expansionist plans.

Increasing Public Discontent

Meanwhile, in the West, there is increasing public intolerance of the views of others or reasonable debate. In the UK, this has applied in Parliament and even media interviewers talk over politicians who's views differ from their own. This would not be tolerated in most other countries. This growing intolerance of other peoples views in public debates is unacceptable, with the one who shouts loudest wins, or so they hope. It seems a short stride to the most powerful being the winner, because "they are right" which justifies violence, the route of all authoritarians. However, these attitudes are also driven by the genuine frustrations of the public, who rightly feel that "Governance" is failing them. Equally, Governments are frustrated that their strategic wishes and manifesto commitments are not being translated into positive end results to the benefit of the public.

Recently, an "intellectual" on a recent BBC programme discussing the NHS, was convinced that the NHS was better than Europe because only 2% of its staff were managers, less than other countries. As a result, he didn't accept that the NHS was inefficient or bureaucratic, a typical conclusion from an inward looking analysis. Dealing with educated people with this narrow, theoretical mentality is an example of the challenges that exist when trying to change state organisations, who do not have the threat of bankruptcy if they do not satisfy the needs of their customers in terms of price and quality of products/services. I have friends who have worked in various public sectors such as prisons, the care sector and the NHS, who have been totally disenchanted with the gross inefficiencies caused by the bureaucracy and have in fact left their jobs. It wasn't money but the disenchantment and lack of job satisfaction that finally drove them out. I would also have left BREL if privatisation hadn't given me a way of breaking out of the "bureaucratic chains".

The following chapters analyse the causes, frustrations and implications of the above, together with the urgent and fundamental change of focus that is needed to improve the performance of democratic institutions and Governments, particularly related to quality of governance, security and economic well being.

2 - THREATS TO DEMOCRACY – GOVERNANCE

Background

Democracy is a relatively new form of Governance, which can take many different forms of electoral representation. However, the administrative arm of Government and the Public Sector Services are critical elements which determine the quality of Governance. Authoritarian regimes have strict, central, bureaucracies, supported by strong military controls, with dissent not being tolerated. These disastrous centralised administrations, together with uncontrolled criminality were prime causes of the public uprisings and financial collapse of the Soviet Union in the 90s.

Early democracies and private companies benefitted from strong central controls during the industrial revolution, when the standards of education were poor and quality and safety standards were high when building Railways, bridges and factories, for example. However, in today's world of rapidly changing technologies and customer expectations, only dynamic and proactive companies survive, meaning that the old bureaucracies, by definition, are a recipe for disaster. Decentralised, customer focussed companies enable success, with responsibility, authority and accountability decentralised more closely to the customer to ensure that products and services meet their requirements.

A classic example of a successful company which structured itself around its products and the needs of its customers, was ABB in the 1990s, a World leading international, multi product engineering company, with only 6 layers from the President to the "shop floor". Turnover was around 60 billion USD at todays values. Many others include Amazon, Google, Apple, Intel, Disney, Samsung, Microsoft, Siemens, Uber and Aldi, whose evolvement and decentralised structures have been based around shaping and meeting the customers needs and has enabled their considerable success. The book Work Rules by Laszlo Bock, the Senior Vice President of People Operations for Google Inc, gives insights from inside Google, which also has only 4 layers from top to bottom. He quotes the example of two T shirt factories in Mexico, one being centrally controlled and the other devolving responsibility. The devolved one was twice as productive, earned higher wages and had 40% lower costs. My own International business was similarly structured, with authority, responsibility and accountability resting with the "local" manager and based around the products/services and satisfying the customers. Compared to the previous centralised organisation, 30% cost improvements were made within the first year with further improvements ongoing. The number of "layers" from top to bottom were reduced by 50%.

Numerous major private companies today are focussed and structured around the customer and use of OKRs (Objectives and Key Results). This is detailed in Appendix 1 by Marcos Barros and also in greater detail in the book that I co authored with him, "Breaking The Chains Of Bureaucracy" (Amazon). However, very few public sectors have replicated this, resulting in the advancement of Democracies compared with Autocracies being limited mainly to the effects of free enterprise, capitalist culture and innovations. Brazil are now following the principles contained in our book and are achieving dramatic (30%) improvements in the quality of public services, with application spreading rapidly across the country, with the support of Marcos. The Civil Servants at all levels are driving this change, because they recognise that it is their responsibility to deliver the services that will satisfy the public. What is stopping other countries.

With Democracy must also come public responsibility, with everybody respecting freedom of expression and establishment of political parties with a range of opposing views. Various academic papers, detailed later in Chapter 3, say that the main internal threats to Democracies are quality of governance, economic strength and security, with populists of the extreme left or right taking electoral advantage of failures in these areas and then reducing the level of democratisation when in power.

From personal global experiences and media generally, the extent of discontent with the quality of governance in democracies generally is higher now than at any time since the end of the Second World War. This has been highlighted by the growth in aggressive demonstrations, with little concern for the impact on others. In addition, growth of extremist parties of the left and right is threatening the democratic process. This is increasingly apparent in several EU countries, Latin America and even the USA, where some Republicans seem to take it as normal to contest the result of any election that they lose. The SNP in Scotland continually agitate for another independence vote, only a few years after the previous "once in a lifetime vote" didn't go their way. With such obsessions, it is hardly surprising that the quality of governance in Scotland is in rapid decline, but the SNP may see the distraction of "independence" as a good way to remove attention from such inconvenient failings. Similar agitations for a return of the UK to the EU will become another distraction or excuse for the EU and UK to be unable to resolve the common underlying failings of Governance and cooperation across both. With the EU given such encouraging "signs" from "rejoiners", then they will continue to try to undermine the UK economy in the hope that the UK will soon return and become one of the largest contributors to the EU economy. This is becoming increasingly important for the struggling EU economy.

Western Democracies cannot afford the luxury of such diversions, when confronted with serious internal Governance failings and external threats.

Analysis of Structural Weaknesses, Conflicts, Responsibilities and Solutions

Fundamental to the success of any Company is the quality of its management/governance. In private Companies this starts with the strategic and management skills and experience of the Chief Executive, Executive Team, and the Controlling Board. The importance of responsiveness to customers, and the type of decentralised organisation structure that will achieve this, is generally now recognised as core to success in the private sector, particularly when needing to respond to rapidly changing technological and environmental challenges. The harsh reality of bankruptcy when not attracting customers tends to focus the mind!

Translating this to the governance of a country, the demands on the expertise of the equivalent "Chief Executive and Executive Management team " are enormous. In democracies, the public usually expect the Prime Minister and his Ministers to perform this role. However, the reality is that it is extremely likely that hardly any of these will have personal experience of managing a large company, even though they could be highly qualified and skilled in other fields. Under such circumstances, their role should become strategic based on the manifesto policies put to the electorate every few years, with success inevitably dependant on the management skills of the permanent Senior Civil Servants, Specialist Advisors and State Sector Executives. These should be made accountable for achieving best practice to satisfy the expectations of the public and value for tax payers' money. The appointment of Senior Civil Servants capable of delivering quality services is the prime responsibility of Ministers. However, the fundamental flaw in the Public Sector centralised organisation structure has to be recognised and addressed by both the Civil Servants, Government Ministers and their Senior Advisors. I had 25 years experiencing the problems of management within a bureaucratic state organisation and then personally managed, with my team, the transition to a decentralised structure, achieving the major improvements within a year. This made it totally clear to me how futile it is to continue with such failing bureaucracies. The fact that we repeated this successful transition and performance improvements in 8 other international state owned businesses shows that it is not rocket science, but absolutely crucial for delivering cost effective customer services.

The prime challenge is to establish efficiency metrics for a State Owned Company, when they do not have competition to establish success in terms of satisfying their customers and winning orders, whilst also delivering profits and positive cash flows for the shareholders/tax payers.

To adopt best international governance standards does not mean mimicking the governance structures of other nations, who also have failing State Sectors, but instead to understand how Private Sector Companies become successful. The collapse of the Soviet Empire and the problems that Putin has experienced in his attack on Ukraine have been partly attributed to centralised control structures, which has contrasted with the devolved power given to the Ukrainian forces, making them more responsive to evolving situations locally. Similar failings applied to Hitler. The economic collapse of the Soviet Union in the 80s was attributable to its centralised and bureaucratic control structure, as was detailed in the recent BBC documentary "Russia- 1985 to 1999". I remember my friend being in Moscow on business at that time and had forgotten to take his underpants. There were none in the shops because "central ordering" had failed, a problem that was not uncommon, as the empty shelves in the shops showed.

This obsession with centralised control, functional departments or "agencies" and resultant failures of governance and customer satisfaction is clearly the responsibility of the senior Civil Service Managers across the Public Sector. They are mandated to efficiently carry out the strategic wishes and policies of the elected government. In addition, the public services provided by the State Sector Management should reflect best international private sector standards and have organisation structures and management skills to meet public expectations of service and value for money. Full responsibility, authority and accountability should be at a level where customers/public can hold those managers to account. The OKR methodology, which is being applied so successfully across Brazil, and by others in the private sector internationally, including Google, should be introduced, starting with a focus onto satisfying public expectations by using metrics to monitor objectives and performance.

The senior Civil Servants should be mandated to deliver results and also to be held accountable by the "Management Board" of Government Ministers. I and most successful Private Sector Managers would take it for granted that bureaucratic organisations are a recipe for disaster. If the Senior Civil Servants do not have the experience of working in large decentralised successful companies, then they do not have that experience to call on. However, if they are unable or unwilling to mentally adjust to and learn from successful private companies such as those listed earlier, and now the state sectors of Singapore and Brazil, then they should resign or be replaced. I am sure that it is not the intellectual capacity that is the issue, but simply the training and indoctrination into one central control philosophy, which has existed for centuries in the Public Sector and now almost becomes an obsession.

Democracy cannot survive if the public loses confidence in the quality of governance as provided by the Public Service. Elected Ministers are unlikely to have the managerial skills to be confident enough to enforce decentralisation of the Public Sector within the 4 year lifetime of a Parliament. A reluctant Civil Service could ensure failure and blame the Government. Being unable to enforce improvements creates a serious failure of trust in the functioning of democratic governance on behalf of the electorate and places the whole credibility of democracy at risk.

In the UK, a recent newspaper survey showed that 40% believe that democracy is failing them. According to International IDEA, "the number of countries moving towards authoritarianism is more than double the number moving towards democracy". Freedom House reports that "a total of 60 countries suffered democratic declines over the past year, while only 25 improved".

Many might say that ministers must accept "executive" responsibility for Governance of a country, in which case I would suggest that most democracies have a fundamentally flawed concept if ministers are being paid little more than doctors or head teachers and only 30% - 50% of senior Civil Servants.

It is clear that executive responsibility for the success or failure of the operational quality and efficiency of public sector governance rests with the senior Civil Servants. The strategic direction of policy rest with the Government, with the support of Specialist Advisors and Senior Civil Servants. Ultimately, the Management Board/Minister, who is representing the tax payer/shareholder, has the responsibility to replace a failing Chief Executive, NOT to assume an executive role with the failing Senior Civil Servant still in position.

Examples of current bureaucratic failures

From my international experience in both the state and private sectors, I have never seen any bureaucratic organisation be successful or dynamic, no matter how good the individual managers. I don't believe that this is the fault of the general employees, who wallow in the morass of coordination and communication meetings, multiple levels of management, functional empires and endless enquiries into why the service has failed. When up to 14 agencies are involved in a "child in need" review meeting for an hour, when little happens except to arrange for a damp and mouldy wall to be repainted rather than resolve the source of damp, then it is clear that something is seriously wrong - an experience that I am personally aware of. This type of failure has also recently resulted in the well publicised death of a 2 year old, caused by mould. Surely one fully responsible child care manager should attend the meeting, who also has the power to instruct other functions/agencies to action as necessary, or has a team with full authority, responsibility and accountability to act.

The Post Office "corruption" scandal of 1998 was a classic example of the consequence of top down management. It started with the common imposition of an all embracing computer system, that was poorly specified and never fit for purpose, but the centre decided it must go ahead to save face, despite warnings up to the most senior levels, including Government, that it was flawed. The consequence was that numerous Post Masters were convicted of fraud, rather than the "establishment" admit their own mistakes, even at the expense of the lives of the Post Masters and their families being ruined. The independent investigation has taken so many years that some have died before being exonerated. Similarly, those responsible could be dead before being held accountable. The man hours and costs associated with this must be staggering, particularly as the cause of the problem was known almost at the outset, but "cover up" seemed to be more important. Within ABB or any private Company, this would have been dealt with within a week.

My own personal experience of this type of "cover up" occurred 20 years ago, when my 92 year old mother died after spending 13 hours on a high trolley in a corridor in A and E, before falling off trying to go to the toilet, breaking her leg and dying. Within 30 minutes of visiting the hospital the next day, I established the facts, including that she had been triaged when she was admitted to hospital and had no fractures or serious ailments. However, over the following days the hospital fabricated the story that her leg was broken before going to the hospital. If so, why was she left on the trolley for 13 hours with no treatment? It took me 2 years to force them to admit the truth, before offering the standard "lessons will be learnt" letter. No acknowledgement that they had deliberately lied to cover up their negligence. I wasn't seeking to sue them but was simply trying to stop it happening to others. My persistence and investigations to establish the truth showed how they managed the hospital and how the functional structure ensured that no one was fully accountable for the patients care except the Chief Executive. The most concerning thing culturally was how the management could create a lie around the cause of death to avoid criticism of individuals. Investigations into failures of governance are too often an expensive exercise in cover up and avoidance of executive responsibility. Many examples of hospital cover ups seem to be emerging regularly now, which raises the question as to whether the NHS is fit for purpose. I feel that it is disastrous that the NHS senior management has allowed such a situation to evolve, when the general calibre and skills of the front end staff are so high. The organisation structure that is imposed on them results in responsibility for patient care spread across many interrelated functions, resulting in easy coordination failures, easy buck passing and no one being held accountable.

The problem of "bed blocking" in hospitals is caused by poor coordination between Community Care and the NHS, each having different ministers and budgets. This "battle" between two closely linked health care facilities is a recipe for disaster which has been responsible for the deaths of many Covid patients. If both were under the control of one Patient Care Manager, having authority, responsibility and accountability for the total care of patients, then this would have been avoided, as would many other coordination problems. However, this book is not about providing detailed solutions to every problem in the state sector. It is focused more on the principles and processes that will firstly establish the requirements of the public and then set clear objectives, actions and results to be achieved to meet their needs. The simplification of organisation and the disciplines around establishing the key metrics to ensure customer satisfaction should be the prime focus. Involvement of local management and staff in establishing these will ensure success, because they know better than anyone the problems and ideal solutions, with, I suggest, guidance from a skilled Consultant.

In the State owned British Railways, this centralised philosophy was also repeated in the materials management stock control system, which my own company was forced to use, which was actually designed to have 8% nil stock items, "because this was the optimum level to achieve the best use of capital"! This resulted in many trains being out of service "waiting materials". Myself and other senior managers tried to persuade the central functional director to change policy, but was told that we were "employed to make things work". Every month, the consequential problems and crisis management action needed to reduce the impact of this, resulted in senior management travelling from around the country for the monthly "crisis" meetings. After privatisation, we changed the system to localise stock control management, including forward planning and eliminated the problem, whilst also reducing stock levels by 70% and material costs by 30%, with no trains out of service waiting materials. All achieved with 1 year and the crisis meetings were no longer needed. In addition the availability of trains for service increased from 72% to 92%. This meant that the newly privatised Train Operating Companies could increase the frequency of services by 30% with no additional investment in new vehicles. The annual cost savings associated with this ran into multi millions of pounds per year.

Another simple example of Governance failure that I am currently experiencing is related to my attempt to obtain a letter from the Inland Revenue to say that I am a UK resident tax payer. One letter followed by 3 phone calls of around 15 minutes each, with promises each time of a reply within 2 weeks has now resulted, after 3 months, of an indication of a reply after another month, although this could stretch to "18 months even". I have been a resident UK tax payer for 62 years, is it so complex? The French even sent a draft letter which needed my personal details to be filled in. The last person that I have spoken to says that he doesn't have the authority to do the reply himself but that I need to speak to a "technician". He said that they have to deal with numerous enquiries without enough staff. Instead of spending 30+ minutes on the phone explaining why they are failing, they could actually spend 5 minutes simply replying to my letter. Ironically, replying to my letter will enable the UK to claim tax from me instead of the French Government. I have finally received a 3 line letter, not in the format requested, confirming my UK residency ,"to the best of their knowledge". This has now been rejected by the French, so I must now start again. These are 2 simple personal examples, but the newspapers are now detailing performance failures daily. This is not a UK only problem, but has now become common across all democracies, with only Singapore and Brazil recognising the cause and the State Sector itself initiating corrective action, without the need for restructuring costs.

How long will it take for the UK and EU Civil Servants to wake up and accept that their inability to resolve these governance failures urgently could rapidly result in the collapse of democracies. The irony is that the new dictatorships of left or right who take over will welcome the bureaucratic central controls and then add military control across the country.

I have never known a private Company repeatedly call for independent enquiries into why it has failed. They would be bankrupt if they had to wait years for the reports to be completed. As the former President of ABB, Perci Barnevic would say, "if a manager doesn't know why his business is failing, then he shouldn't be a manager". This automatically applies to football managers, why not in the state sector? Unfortunately the cry is "I want more money" or it "wasn't me it was them" or "lessons will be learnt", with no one being held accountable.

The purpose of recounting these examples is to try to highlight how the failures of governance caused by bureaucracy has widespread implications, not only on the cover up culture and quality of service, but also the huge implications on both the public and the direct and indirect knock on effects on the total cost of the services. Furthermore, the impact on the self esteem of dedicated employees, who become trapped into these cultures of self indulgence by senior management is little short of scandalous. So many excellent employees grasp the opportunity to leave such unfulfilling jobs.

Organisation Solution and Benefits

Without fail, every state sector operation that my company acquired in various countries, was bureaucratic but transformed with 30% improvement in cost and service levels within a year and with minimal input of external staff. The transition needed specialist support in the first year to ensure that the correct focus, process and metrics were rigorously established, with no short cuts. 12 layers of management would be reduced to 5, with focus onto excellence of service to the public resulting in employees proud of their performance and company.

It is the senior Civil Servants, who should be coming forward to Governments with a proposal to refocus onto their customers by decentralising and delayering their Organisations, making them "fit for purpose". It is unrealistic to think that the Prime Minister or a Minister is going to do their job for them. Within such structures, in order to achieve change, clear guidance and commitment from the top is essential, with facilitation by an experienced consultant usually being necessary. This was the way, in 2020, for the first successful application in the public sector in Brazil. An experienced senior Civil Servant, Sabrina Baes, was so enthused at a presentation by Marcos Barros to Companies in Brazil, that she requested his help in refocussing the management of her Public Sector.

In 2022 I was asked, with Marcos Barros, to make presentations at an "OKR Public Sector Conference" of around 700 senior managers in Brazil, with the aim of spreading this major success story and concept across the Country. It now has many new converts and is being spread rapidly, with Marcos being the guiding force together with Sabrina. This was also the approach that I used within my own Company. Success breeds success and creation of "Centres of Excellence" helps a company to spread best practice, with the successful international company ABB being a prime example in the 1990s. An even larger Conference is now planned for 2023 to benefit the whole of Brazil as rapidly as possible. Both Marcos and myself live in the UK and have offered free advice to the UK Government, but have been told that they are already doing this! Where?

These excellent senior mangers in the State of Matto Grosso do Sul in Brazil recognise the need to optimise the quality of services to the public, by breaking through the constraints of functional organisations. They are taking the initiative to accept responsibility for the quality of service of their sector/departments. They are not waiting for the Government to tell them what to do or how to do it. They recognise that they are being paid to do that job. They are not crying out for more money/resources, they are focussing on optimising what is achievable with what they have and the public are the beneficiaries. The public sector employees that I met were also rightly proud of their achievements. The same applied within my own company as we devolved responsibilities, authority and accountability. In fact, Private companies in Brazil are also asking Marcos to apply the OKR customer focussed process to their businesses. The speed and scale of improvements make it inevitable that it will ultimately be applied internationally. In Sweden, they are facing up to the major problems within their Health Sector and we have shared our experiences with the project leader tasked with seeking a solution. Hopefully, they will be successful.

Role and Challenges of Elected Ministers

As previously stated, some say that Government Ministers

should have the ability to be able to take full executive management responsibility for the Public Sector. If so, they need to have the appropriate skills and managerial experience. How do you attract top quality and experienced managers to become elected representatives who can also control and manage a huge company/public sector of £1 trillion turnover (UK)? They must firstly try to be picked as an MP, win a seat at an election, hope that their party wins that election and hope that they are not replaced at the next one, 4 years later. The Civil Servants know this and can easily put up a barricade of "severe consequences" if any attempt is made to change the status quo. I was offered such an "opportunity" to be an MP in the early stages of my career, but decided it would be a financial sacrifice and risk that I couldn't afford. In addition, even then, 40 years ago, the intrusive nature of the media into politicians lives made the whole thing seem highly unattractive. Any story, true or false, has already ruined the lives of many public figures. Some countries prevent such media intrusions. Others say that the public should know every aspect of the character of their elected representatives. However, a "perfect" person, which doesn't exist, would not understand what real life is about.

Some countries, such as France, seem to have a specialist academic route for "politicians", and likewise for civil servants, but again I would question their ability to represent the public if their experience of the real world is so limited. This type of evolvement also ensures that change is limited, with the same old practices enduring. However, exposure to a competitive environment where failure has severe consequences ensures that striving for best practice and customer satisfaction are fundamental for success. Or you follow the Brazilian route where in house public sector managers are fully aware of the functional organisational deficiencies and want to grasp the opportunity to make changes for the benefit of the public. This will allow elected politicians in Brazil to focus on strategic issues rather than continually "fire fighting" local public service failures and complaints.

In order to overcome some of the challenges that MPs face, some countries seem to accept, or turn a blind eye to the fact that politicians will receive "recompense" in other "unofficial" ways, or after leaving politics altogether. Hardly a way to impress the public. The reality is that Governance is seen as a serious problem across all democracies, but the cause should not be seen simply as a failure of either the MPs or employees in the Public Sector. It is my belief, certainly in the UK, that most politicians are involved because they want to make an improvement to their community and country. However they, together with Public Sector employees, are frustrated with the constraints of their organisation and loss of credibility in the eyes of the public. They need a leader who will recognise the core problem and drive the change, like Sabrina in Brazil and, may I say, myself and my team in my privatised company.

Summary

Accepting the reality of the challenge facing Government Ministers, in order to make democracy work, then the onus of responsibility for delivering high quality Public Services must, I repeat, rest with the Civil Service. Firstly, the Civil Service Management must be held accountable for carrying out the wishes of the Government. They should also be made to account directly to the public and media for the performance of their departments. Some countries such as New Zealand work this way. In this rapidly changing world, current senior managers will have started careers with mobile phones the size of bricks and fax machines being the means of messaging. Ironically I have just received a letter from HMRC with a fax number on it! I didn't have a TV until I was 9. In 1960 only 5% of students went to university, today it is 50%. The Public Sector training and development programmes were excellent, as I experienced, but much was wasted because the centralised and bureaucratic organisation structure, which was orientated towards a poorly educated workforce, constrained initiatives at lower levels and change was considered to be a risk and discouraged. In essence, the skills and pride of the employees were not recognised.

My own career covered 25 years in the public sector before privatisation. Subsequently I was involved with public sectors around the world, including being responsible for acquisitions of their operations and transforming them by focussing on satisfying the customers. All had the same top heavy, multi layered bureaucracies. This necessitated organisation change, with significant value added and customer service improvements.

Details of how this was achieved, and the commonality of all public sector organisations around the world in terms of bureaucracy and inefficiency are contained in the book "Breaking The Chains Of Bureaucracy" (Amazon), which I wrote with co author Marcos Barros, an International Management Consultant. I do not intend to repeat the contents of that book here, but ask you to accept that the inefficiencies and constraints inherent in bureaucracies result in customer/public dissatisfaction and enormous waste of money. If you have any doubts, please read the book, which also details the change process which becomes fully effective within a year. We wrote the book in the hope that Governments would respond and improve the governance of democracies. I also felt that sharing my team's unique life time of experiences could dramatically reduce the developing debt crisis, but maybe the "not invented here syndrome" and the need for another "special commission" could make sure that it is kicked into the long grass, with the danger that no one except democracy itself being held "accountable" by the public. Brazil and Singapore have shown the way.

To summarise, the public is increasingly disillusioned with the quality of public services, with the increasing trend of populists of left or right taking control of Governments. This will accelerate the demise of democracies unless the "Chains of Bureaucracy" are broken. If the current Senior Civil Servants do not recognise the need for rapid organisation change, then the Government must appoint a new experienced leadership who will ensure that a proactive team will drive the change. The process of change is not rocket science, does not involve massive investment, but achieves proven 30% performance improvements within 1 year. It is happening progressively across Brazil, has happened in Singapore, and has been done by myself in the UK, Europe and Africa. More recently Amazon and Google have applied the organisation principles to enable their formidable success, Aldi has created its success by orientating its focus around the customer and most other large private companies use the same structures. The use of

OKRs (Objectives and Key Results) is rapid and places local management and customer service at the heart of the process, whilst also breaking through bureaucracy. The core elements for success are an enthusiastic and committed leader and proactive team, with experienced guidance. The employees embrace the changes as common sense and "about time to"!

Historically, when the general public were poorly educated, centralised bureaucracies gave stability and consistency, today it provides annoyance, poor service and frustration. The Democratic leaders were generally admired 100 years ago, but it is difficult to identify one who is today. We have actors, comedians, lawyers and writers amongst others. Junker, the Prime Minister of Luxembourg, one of the smallest countries in the world, was appointed President of the European Commission, the administrative arm of one of the largest trading and currency zones in the world. Central control and bureaucracy increased. The USA has a 78 year old President, with Trump his alternative. Many EU countries are having populist movements of right and left demonstrating against their Governments, plus a military coup attempt in Germany, whilst others are electing extremist leaders. Bureaucracy is stifling the performance of the vast majority of Public Services. In essence, centralised bureaucracies are, by definition, led by an autocratic style of leadership, hence the reason that they are used by Autocrats. This conflict of interests at the heart of democracies will ultimately tear democracies apart.

On what basis does any State Sector Manager deny the tax payers, who pay their salaries, of the chance to have better Health Care, for example, or the chance to have a reduction in tax rather than an increase. No risk is involved because the process of transforming organisations and performance is so well proven.

A wake up call is urgently needed, before the current slow decline of democratisation escalates into a collapse and a new era of competing autocracies.

3 - THREATS TO DEMOCRACY – SECURITY

International

Security includes both external international threats and internal personal ones which include criminal gangs, drug barons and petty crime. "Defence of a Country" is a prime responsibility of all Governments, and the "West", post Second World War, was eager to welcome both Russia and China into the international trading community, in the hope that they would also embrace democracy and denounce further conflict. It is a fact of life and history that power obsessed authoritarians, sometimes under the cloak of religion, are the prime cause of international aggression and wars. Democracies have generally shown a respect for other peoples views, including international laws.

However, optimism and wishful thinking seemed to overcome realism, and the West dropped its guard in the euphoria of the 90s. With the collapse of the Soviet Union and in the belief and hope that Russia would be democratised, the West started to reduce the NATO forces in Europe. This was in spite of the fact that Russia was becoming a lawless country, controlled by criminal gangs, drugs barons and oligarchs. Democracy was collapsing with elections being manipulated to the extent that they became meaningless. Putin from the KGB was then made leader, by manipulation of the media and propaganda. True democracy was finished and the country was a dictatorship under the control of Putin with compliant oligarchs. After the collapse of the economy and rule of law, the Russian people could only see improvements and they could also see a leader intent on recreating the Soviet Empire, with Crimea following Chechnya. They ignored the fact that the wealth of the country was being diverted into the pockets of Putin and his Oligarchs. It was better than the previous collapse into lawlessness and bankruptcy.

During this period, the West was also hoping that China, which appeared to be introducing a capitalist culture on the East Coast, would then spread this further across the country, together with democratisation, which could bring an enormous new market for the West. In the interim and in order to encourage this market, it appeared that the West was prepared to ignore the enforcement of international law such as Intellectual Property and Human Rights. All the signs were there at the turn of the century that this was a dangerous strategy. The consequence has been that these two large authoritarian countries have been allowed to grow in economic and military strength, with Russia becoming a major supplier of energy resources to Europe and Germany in particular. Also China has been allowed to become a major supplier of critical rare earths (71%) and products for infrastructure, computers and high technology products including security systems, as well as being a cheap source of products generally which has undermined Western manufacturing industries.

Surely a key element of security planning is to never be dependant on strategically critical supplies from a potential enemy, particularly an authoritarian one who, by its nature, inevitably has an obsession with power. Furthermore, what type of narcissist might step in as the successor. How many authoritarian powers historically have been passive? "Power Corrupts" is not a meaningless phrase, and the search for "benevolent dictators" can be challenging and they will always be vulnerable to a more aggressive replacement. Even today, China is taking a stake in another European Port, this time Hamburg and Germany and France are also currently seeking to expand trade links with China, in the hope, no doubt, of offsetting their struggling economies. However, how much further exposure to autocracies will they risk before they dangerously expose the whole EU economy to them. Does the EU President, the President of Foreign Affairs or the

President of Finance have a strategic view on this? Why didn't the EU sanction Germany, France and the other seven EU countries for selling arms to Russia after the embargo on arms sales was imposed after their annexation of Crimea? After the USA and UK, why is Poland the largest EU supplier of arms to Ukraine, contributing 4 times more than France in the critical first 6 months of the war? The plea by the EU is that it can only contribute 1% of GDP to NATO instead of the agreed 2%, owing to its economic problems. If the US considers that Europe is abusing its economic support to security in Europe, then withdraws that support, as Trump threatened, then the EU will have no option but to urgently increase its defence expenditure before Russia retakes its former Empire and even more.

The USA and UK, through NATO, have once again become the guardians of European security by stopping Putin marching across EU countries. Unfortunately, this has been at the expense of the UK economy, which will look less healthy than those countries who have under invested in NATO. Western Democracies have become complacent and self absorbed, with younger generations and populists seeking new levels of idealism, whilst seeking to ridicule, despise and disown those heroes of the past who fought for the survival of their families, country and democracy in the only way known at that time. To try to make a nation ashamed of its heritage or to denigrate individuals who lived in a totally different era and culture, is to do the propaganda work of today's authoritarian aggressors. It is no coincidence that the extreme left and right provides support to such populist groups. Denigration of those who sacrificed their lives or were successful in building a military strength to survive against repeated attacks by neighbours, appears to be today's "noble" target to disinherit. Failure to be interested in understanding their forefathers situation, such as "attack or be attacked" is now typical of a new idealistic generation, who have never experienced fear of attack, torture, genocide, the destruction of homes and families or even the cause or implications of a country's economic collapse and enslavement by a foreign power. Putin's treatment of Ukraine and its people should be a wake-up call.

The nuclear threats by Putin and replication of Hitler's

strategies and rhetoric, shows that the world is still relatively primitive in its instincts. Idealism, however noble, should never be at the expense of both short and long term survival. Whilst Russia's actions has brought NATO together, China has been far more strategic in its manoeuvring to achieve global power. It has increased "western" economic dependancy on its products to the extent that the strategy of NATO countries towards China is beginning to fragment. China is encouraging this by favouring the gullible at the expense of the more aware. The economic fragility of Western countries is already ensnaring Germany and France to be rushing to China to secure new trade deals, ignoring its non compliance with international standards and laws. This is somewhat in conflict with their treatment of the UK, the second largest NATO supporter, which must give encouragement to China.

The financial weakness of democracies, and the desperation to find a solution, is the prime reason for this entrapment. Returning to the core arguments of the previous chapter; fortunately, this can be overcome by reducing the enormous waste of resources currently tied up in the inefficient Public Sector bureaucracies of all Democracies. The Senior Civil Servants of NATO countries should now be recognising that they have a prime responsibility to safeguard democracies across the world against a collapse into the chaos of individual autocracies, leaving exposure to the march of China. China is relying on the fact that Civil Servants, who have established an enormously powerful grip on democracies, will, like themselves, be reluctant to relinquish that power. The weakness of democracies, with elections every few years, as discussed earlier, will result in the all powerful central establishment resisting pressure to change from "transient" ministers. Dominic Cummings attempted and failed and other Ministers who try to improve performance are accused of bullying. This type of environment will kill democracies. The Civil Servants responsible should be held to account by the media. Rather than helpless ministers being pilloried, these Civil Servants should be challenged to explain why they are not adopting best practice to rectify the disastrous Public Services.

Evolvement of Introverted "Bubbles of Idealism"

The lack of international security awareness and fear in democracies has been replaced by introspection and intolerance of other people's views. Pressure groups have become micro authoritarians in their own special cocoons. This attitude is also being enhanced by the use of algorithms to implant subtle "propaganda" through the internet, which effectively builds on the prejudices that may only mildly exist. This can ultimately build into anger, hate and blind prejudice. What action is being taken to stop such manipulations, which is inevitably now a powerful tool of autocracies, democracies and companies? In the UK, the media is now accused of a subtle undercurrent of shaming "Britishness". This intolerance has already become common across all aspects of democratic debate, be it Remainers or Brexiteers, Labour or Conservatives, net zero within 30 years, or is it 8 now? The merit of differing views should be respected to allow the search for realistic targets which do not threaten national economies, security or even existence in the event of nuclear war.

Democracies mean nothing unless they strive for greater social awareness and respect for each other and listen to reasoned debate. Intolerance of any alternative views or even modifications means that democracy, by definition, is under threat and only the strongest will prevail. Currently, blocking roads, stopping trains, trying to deface statues or museums and stopping others earning a living is a form of authoritarian behaviour and undermines the legitimate right to protest. The take over of Universities by populists or minorities is also a disturbing development, when they should be havens of free thinking and debate. Blocking local fracking, oil exploration or nuclear plants and then leaving dictators such as Putin to easily destroy our economy, leaving us vulnerable to attack by him, is naive in the extreme, particularly as he will continue to produce and use pollutants and we, of necessity, will buy them until alternatives are available. Tolerance of internal intolerance within democracies, when surrounded by aggressive dictators, is a recipe for disaster. Democracies cannot accept internal authoritarianism, as occurred in Germany with Hitler. The poor quality of governance generally is fostering this dangerous discontent.

The move of the world to a green environment is laudable and necessary, but needs realism and openness to debate as to how best to achieve this without being destroyed in the process. Being a self righteous "green" at home, but to then buy the same "polluting" products from "non green" countries is hypocritical and self destructive. I believe that demands for "restitution" from "polluting" countries to those affected by environment change is somewhat tenuous. Who is to say who started the pollution? Those who chopped down trees for wood to keep warm, cook, make tools and pots and developed medicines to double life expectancy were the forerunners, but equally those who purchased such items, whilst extending their own life expectancy were also encouraging the growth of pollutants! I believe that it is better not to enter into meaningless blame or reward games but to encourage a global supportive culture to those in trouble. But those who do not support control of emissions should be excluded from selling products freely into global markets. The current strategy seems to favour current polluters at the expense of the rest, who are trying to control emissions. However, the purpose of this book is not to provide solutions to the problems of the world, but to preserve democratic freedoms and debate to enable best solutions for both individuals and nations.

Globalisation in a fully democratised world is laudable. Even to encourage authoritarian regimes to voluntarily become democratised by incorporating them into a new free trading world is understandable, provided that they abide by the United Nations rules. However, to allow such a strategy to continue for 75 post war years has simply resulted in the extreme authoritarian regimes, such as Russia and China, to become the most dangerous military forces in the world. With China in particular having been allowed to not comply with UN rules such as Intellectual Property Rights and Human Rights, this has now resulted in them growing to become a leading world economic power, who have also placed many poorer countries and strategic ports into vulnerable situations with loans and penal debt default terms. Furthermore, China is now responsible for 25% of the worlds pollutants and democracies such as Germany and France are currently seeking to expand trade links with them even further. China will encourage this, driving a wedge between NATO countries. The so called green democracies will be winning COP awards as their economies shrink, resulting in their democracies being overthrown. Meanwhile, China expands its economic influence, pollutes and destroys large swathes of the world without use of military force.

Rise of Populism, Decline of Democracy

Responsibility for this must rest with the major democracies who have allowed shorter term economic advantages to dominate over longer term security. With Western Democracies adopting such a trusting approach to unpredictable Autocracies and narcissists, it is understandable that the idealism of the younger generation seeks to focus on perceived injustices, racialism, sexuality and also the major concern of climate change. However, this new addiction of "self righteousness" and creating an "ideal world" appears to be crippling rational analysis and debate, with increasingly strident behaviour and intolerance of dissension. Proper evaluation of the best actions to achieve strategic goals optimises the chance of success. Would private companies allow inexperienced junior staff to bully and dictate the direction of the Company? This would now appear to be the default position of many democracies. Consequently, populism has increased across the world, with extreme left or right wing leaders gaining in popularity. The consequence must be an increased risk to global security. Some have even aligned themselves in support of Putin, but others have backed away as he appears to be losing control.

In the Research Group Freedom House 2019 report titled Democracy in Retreat, it showed that "freedom of expression was in retreat" over the previous 13 years with sharper drops since 2010. This was particularly noticeable in Hungary, Poland, Czech Republic, Turkey, Brazil, Venezuela and India.

A 2018 analysis by political scientists Yascha Mount and Jordan Kyle links populism to democratic backsliding. Since 1990, it found that out of 13 right wing populist governments and 15 left wing populist governments, 5 of each showed significant democratic "back sliding".

A 2018 report by the Tony Blair Institute For Global Change

also concluded that populist rule of left or right leads to "significant risk of democratic backsliding". They conclude that populist governments are 4 times more likely to cause harm to democratic institutions than non populist governments, attacking individual rights, such as press freedoms, civil liberties and political rights. However, Populists gain power by "articulating genuine societal demands and pushing issues of good governance".

Concerning quality of governance relating to internal security at home and crime generally, the failure of policing in terms of investigating crimes and prosecution successes is a cause for serious concern. Drug and gang related crime is now a serious problem, with young people being recruited by such gangs. This dangerous underworld is becoming increasingly prevalent across the world, resulting in "no go" areas and requires urgent action. The failure to control it accelerated the collapse of the attempt at democracy in Russia in the 90s.

The security and legal services appear to be unfit for purpose, with prosecution rates being low and cases taking many months and even a year to come to court. Lack of public confidence in the police and legal services is another cause for disenchantment and will be another "tool" for the populists to use to stir up public unrest. These services need the systems analysis of OKRs to be used, as in Brazil, to optimise the focus and resources more effectively. Confidence in security internally and externally are the bedrock of a nation. In addition, analysis of best practices in other countries should be unashamedly analysed and adopted if appropriate. Low level policing in France, for example, handles parking and local policing, whilst the Gendarmerie handles more serious crimes. Similarly, much could be learnt by German and French health services. Fortunately, Intellectual Property Laws do not apply to such matters, but for some reason the Public Sectors of democracies appear not to be interested to take advantage of this "free experimentation". The private sector and China have worked hard to apply global best practice/technology.

Lack of resources and funds are frequent excuses for poor performance, but gross inefficiencies can easily be overcome by following the OKR/ decentralisation process and best practice as used in many countries and companies.

4 - THREATS TO DEMOCRACY – ECONOMIC

Since the Second World War, democracies have seen dramatic improvements to the quality of life, health and relative wealth.

The 50s saw TVs become widespread, together with shared phone lines. The 60s saw cars become more widespread, even to me as a student. Only 5% went to university and Jazz was phased out to be replaced by pop concerts and the Beatles. Whilst the 70s was plagued by industrial unrest, restrictive practices and with much of the UK being state owned and loss making, the country was in severe financial difficulties with high inflation and interest rates. However the 80s saw a revival with Thatcher and mass privatisations, which revitalised financial performance and a focus onto customer satisfaction. Foreign holidays became even more common. The 90s onwards saw an explosion in new technologies such as mobile phones, computers, internet, websites and robotics. Economic growth allowed wages growth to outpace inflation and with low unemployment, the public felt a sense of well being. Life expectation had increased and health care had improved and 50% of children went to university. Democratisation was spreading rapidly.

Stalling Economic Growth

The early 2000s saw the terrorist attack on New York and the response against Iraq. Terrorism became a common threat and East Mediterranean countries became increasingly involved in conflicts. 2007 saw the financial crises, which brought a halt to significant economic growth. Financial manipulations enabling countries to continue drifting along without facing up to serious structural problems, has resulted in steadily increasing debt to GDP ratios. In a private company, rather than turning to borrowing for survival, urgent focus would have firstly turned to potential for internal efficiencies. The public are fully aware of the deterioration in the quality of service from all Public Services and also the serious administrative failures that are constantly highlighted by the media, together with a growth in national debts. Unemployment rates in the EU were high, particularly for the young. The COVID crisis then badly impacted global trade and the Russian attack on Ukraine has badly affected both trade, energy supplies and inflation and is throwing many countries into a recession.

With public services continuing to deteriorate whilst also demanding more from tax payers as the only solution, sympathy and tolerance with the performance of Public Services across all democracies was reaching a break point, with public demonstrations and strikes increasing and extremist parties gaining in popularity as the public desperately sought a solution. Critically, western economies are struggling to withstand the economic effect of Putin's attack on Ukraine, which is now compounding the previous economic frailties, with inflation, interest rates, energy and trading problems directly impacting on both the economic resilience of democracies and effectively reducing the real buying power of the public. The consequence of this can be irrational public behaviour, as they strike out in desperation. Political Parties globally are taking the blame, but this book is highlighting the prime source of the problem as being the bureaucratic public sector organisations and their senior managers, who, of course, are ultimately responsible to Governments.

Applying the proven restructuring successes, as described earlier, would rapidly overcome both the national and individual economic problems and disillusionment with Governance.

Centralised, bureaucratic, multi layered organisations are notoriously inflexible and inefficient and in a rapidly changing world are not used by successful private companies. Anyone who has worked in them know the struggle to achieve even a half decent performance. With numerous examples of the scope for savings/ service improvements being of the order of 30%, then the the public are becoming increasingly angry at the failure of Government and the Public Sector to even admit that they have a problem. With the public sector in democracies representing 40-60% of GDP, then it is apparent that action to reduce debts by improving Public Sector efficiency could avoid the large interest rate and tax increases that are going to cause recessions and further financial hardship. The public reaction could be volatile, particularly if civil servants go ahead with threatened strike action. Can they truly be unaware of their failure of Governance? The serious implications on global security and democracy itself has been dealt with in previous chapters.

The reality is that all of this could be avoided if senior Civil Servants would accept and address their own organisation deficiencies and take immediate action to decentralise their structures. The public cries of anguish at £50 billion spending cuts and tax increases would be dwarfed by the £300 billion potential savings in the UK, for example, or even a declaration that a plan is in place to make this happen progressively over a couple of years. When we have UK specialists helping Brazil to transform their services across the country, and also being the lead participants in a large conference of senior Public Sector Managers in Brazil, why is it so difficult for the UK to ask them to do the same in the UK? Calling a meeting with senior officials could at least explore the possibilities of achieving a similar dramatic transformation, not only in the quality of governance and economic performance of the UK, but also the financial hardship that so many are soon to suffer. The full implications of this on global democracies is currently unknown, but will certainly be negative,

Aggressive autocracies such as Russia, China, Iran and North Korea, are aware of the Governance problems in democracies and are most likely fostering public discontent through social media and algorithms, which could also be encouraging them to become increasingly aggressive. As a result of the West's dependence on rare raw materials and high tech components from China, manufacture of core products and systems could be brought to a stand still, particularly if the West decided to oppose China's declared expansionist plans, not only in Asia but globally. With many small countries committed to debt repayments to China, with penal terms of repossession in the event of default, it can be seen that China is near to establishing a strangle hold over the world.

Solutions

Time is fast running out for the West to act. Senior Civil Servants have the chance to either save democracies or sink them by burying their heads in the sand. Failure to act should result in immediate replacement.

The potential for Western Democracies to respond is severely limited with the current Governance structures. The fact that only 50% of military equipment is available for use in Germany, one of the most "efficient" countries, shows that urgent action is needed. With potentially large efficiency improvements in Public Sectors, the release of some of this money into productive and innovative private sectors could transform dependency on unpredictable autocracies. Potentially this equates to 12-20% of GDP which would transform the performance of most democracies, whose debt is now soaring above 100% of GDP.

The continual financial manipulations of the finance sector, whilst creative in its own way in an emergency, is no substitute for good, dynamic management as the means to create economic security and growth. Any successful large private sector company knows this. In reality, democracies have used the low wage countries such as China to support increasingly inefficient and self serving governance structures, which were designed for autocracies and the industrial revolution. When private companies use "creative" accountancy to doctor their financial figures, then you know that serious problems could be ahead. The false magic and freedoms perceived with the creation of a bureaucratic, central controlling eurozone could ultimately be a noose around the neck of member countries, unless they all understand the need to improve both the quality and efficiency of their governance. Already it can be seen that the productivity engine room of Germany is faltering, with the lower valued euro making life "easy" for German exports in the early years. They then nurtured the "easy" Russian market, even though Putin has been stating his expansionist intentions for 15 years, becoming dependent on it rather than working harder to find wider more reliable markets. Consequently Germany has declined and is entrapped by an aggressive autocracy. It now appears to be reaching out to China!

Freedom of movement in the EU is also resulting in the poorer new members losing both their younger and skilled people to the higher paying EU countries. Instead of driving their own training and growth strategies through good governance, they accept the easy short term do nothing option, which will ultimately undermine their own economies and will also undermine the poorer countries. This was a fatal trap that the UK fell into when it opened its doors to the new low wage EU members 20 years ago. The UK, as always, was first to apply the EU free movement rules enthusiastically, whilst the rest of the EU followed a few years later, like the blind leading the blind, with all resulting in lower wage, low growth economies over the subsequent 10-15 years.

With the EU itself also being governed by a strong, controlling, central bureaucracy in Brussels, it is difficult to envisage the process for organisation change in the EU, particularly with the common currency. It can be done by accepting some hard truths that all member countries will be better served by a common trading block with independent currencies, rather than an obsessive drive for a Federal State with even greater central controls. The election of a more extreme right wing government in Italy is a warning of the extent of public dissatisfaction, which is increasingly apparent in many other countries including France. The fact that a military coup could recently be attempted in Germany, or that Trump could be accused of encouraging a public attack on the Whitehouse in the 2020s is difficult to believe.

Economically strong countries, with the public experiencing the feel good factor, would not experience such behaviour. Economic weakness results in Governments taking short term actions which could undermine long term security, as outlined previously.

5 - THREATS TO DEMOCRACY - BEHAVIOUR AND COMPETENCE

Fundamental to the credibility and reputation of any democratic government is the respect that it earns as a result of the behaviour and integrity of its politicians, together with the competence and quality of its Governance. Democracies allow the public to have an avenue to express their views. However, I believe that this also requires the public and media to act responsibly when allowed freedom of expression. In the UK, there appears to be a constant propaganda campaign by the "opposition" media from day one against the Party in power. Ultimately this must become extremely debilitating for the Government and could also undermine the credibility of democracy itself, particularly if a populist seizes on this continual denigration of democratic parties and their representatives and uses the solution of authoritarian control, which then bans a free media. On the other hand, integrity in both Governance and media is something that should be demanded. It is interesting to watch Euronews and France 24 News, which are focussed on extracting information from guests on a wider range of topics, whereas on UK TV news channels, presenters obsess on one topic endlessly, whilst also asking long winded loaded questions aimed at undermining the politician. Of course, politicians must be challenged, but in reality the main causes of public discontent are related to the poor performance of the Public Services, so it is the fully responsible and accountable Civil Servant, if one exists, who should be challenged directly by the media. This actually happens in New Zealand to a far greater degree. In Autocracies, in total contrast, it is common for the leader and senior cabal of "oligarchs" to be amongst the richest in the world and public dissent is quashed with force if necessary, with media strictly controlled by the State. Corruption at many levels is also common, but turning a blind eye is also a means of ensuring broader compliance.

Behaviour and competence are far more difficult subjects to quantify, because they deal with basic human frailties, culture and prejudices, which vary across countries and organisations. It is easy to gloss over these because of their complexity. However, these could well be another core reason that democracies ultimately fail. Politicians who abuse the trust and power that they are given has a debilitating impact on public respect and makes it easier for populists and the media to stir up discontent against the establishment. However, the alternative consequential authoritarian regimes allow for even greater abuse of power without penalty. The rise to power in authoritarian regimes will be the result of certain personal characteristics of the leader, and will also require manipulation and ruthlessness, and to maintain power will need continual strict central control of all functions including the military. The fear of being usurped is strong and the price for loyalty can be high. The culture in many authoritarian regimes results in side payments being normalised, but in addition, the macho or narcissistic nature of the leader is a "norm" that is accepted by the public, particularly if the country is respected as an international power capable of both defending itself and expanding its territory, but propaganda and fear are also powerful controllers of the public.

However, democratic political parties need to be able to respond to the mood of the electorate and improve their quality of life. In addition they should preferably earn their respect to be re-elected, rather than being the "least worst"option. The quality of governance, security, the quality of life and continual improvements in living standards and public services are all expected by the public. Delivering on election promises gives credibility. Lack of integrity is frowned upon by many countries but is almost accepted by others as inevitable, with little difference compared to dictatorships. In France, when asking about the frequent prosecution of Mayors, a shrug of the shoulders and sadly "c'est normal" is a common response. However, countries do have strict rules against corruption which are rigorously applied. In the UK, over 25 years, I was only once offered a small gift from a company after they had been awarded a contract, which I declined. Irrespective of the moral issue, I had observed the threat of blackmail that can arise when going down such a path. Internationally, unfortunately, the culture was rather different in some countries and became a sad reflection on the integrity inherent in those democratic countries, who were failing the trust of the public.

Looking more deeply into the calibre of politicians, in the UK most would appear to have a genuine concern to serve their constituency to the best of their ability. Some are career politicians who follow a narrow path with the aim of being an MP, whilst others follow various careers before focussing on being an MP. The strength of Parliament is having MPs with a wide range of experiences who can give voice to them in parliament. However, the fundamental core to successful Governance is to have a State Administration and Public Sector that has the flexibility and ability to respond to both strategic issues and local requirements. From considerable personal experience, I know that the challenge isn't the competence of the employees generally, but the framework and constraints in which they operate.

My career evolved in the Railway Workshops state sector, and I spent the first 4 years at University whilst also gaining experience working on the shop floor and in various office functions. The commitment, motivations and frustrations of all employees stayed with me for life. The senior managers of the many centralised functions in such state sectors had no idea of the impact that some of their decision making had on the ultimate company performance in terms of internal efficiency and poor customer experiences. Even when confronted with facts, they would insist that the lower levels should resolve the problems that they were causing! After progressing up the management structure over 20 years, managing in various functions such as production, development, industrial relations, planning and works management, I realised that to bring about meaningful change or improvements for both the Company and customers was virtually impossible unless the remote functional decision makers were removed or made to work at the "front end" in order to experience the consequences of their decisions.

Finally, privatisation enabled me to call on my years of experience to then implement a more dynamic, customer focused and decentralised organisation that resulted in 30% performance improvement and supplier of "first resort" instead of "last resort", all within one year. Without those years of management experience in multi layered management tiers and endless communication and liaison meetings, I would have found it difficult to push confidently for a new "Product" based organisation that was focussed around the customers. In the 80's, I wasn't aware of a reference or "model" to follow, but I did have a team who were equally frustrated and were sufficiently experienced to know that moving management controls of all functions locally could dramatically improve efficiency and customer service. I had no problem in convincing everyone in my works of the benefits of this devolvement. They responded each year with continual improvement initiatives across the total range of governance, from supplier management, cash flow, quality, delivery and reliability improvements that were impossible for me to have initiated through central diktat, in spite of my experience.

Short Termism of Democracies - Solutions

The reality is that elected Governments must have fears that if they try to force a "negative" Civil Service into decentralising their structures, then they could deliberately make it fail resulting in the elected government being voted out at the next election within a maximum of 4 years time. The new Government would then be reluctant to risk the same approach. This is why the Senior Civil Servants must take ownership for the restructuring of their organisations. If they are not committed then they should leave.

If the decline in democratisation is to be stopped, this almost "authoritarian" control by the Civil Service/ Public Sector must be overcome. The reality is, however, that politicians, who have no personal experience of handling such an organisation transition, must recruit new leaders in the State Sector who are committed to the change, or do as Brazil has done and identify enthusiastic leaders who are committed to the philosophy and enlist the help of experienced consultants to facilitate the change. A Centre of Excellence can then be established allowing others to visit, observe and gain confidence in the process of change. My experience of implementing these changes in various countries is that the scale of performance improvements make interim "support" costs insignificant compared to the benefits. In addition, the many consultants who were employed across various failing sectors of the company became unnecessary.

To conclude, competence is not the prime problem in the pubic sector generally, except, perhaps, with long serving managers who have been indoctrinated into a cultural environment of functions and many management layers, where coordination, communication and investigations into repeated failures becomes a way of life. It can be difficult for such managers to accept that a lifetimes management approach may not be the best in today's environment. They should be given the respect that they deserve, but if incapable of change, they should be offered early retirement, voluntary redundancy or transfer to a position that is more appropriate for them. However, I found that such self doubts became non issues under the waves of dramatic performance improvements. In Brazil, some managers had initial reservations that were rapidly dispelled when the improved performance became evident and they then became drivers of change.

I was the senior catalyst for change in my company as was Sabrina Baes in Brazil, who responded to an OKR Conference led by Marcos Barros in Mato Grosso Do Sul. She was also fortunate to have the support of other open minded senior managers who supported the drive to implement the philosophy nationally, through the recent OKR Public Sector Conference in Campo Grande, with 700 participants. This has resulted in further expansion including Brasilia, to be followed next year with an even larger conference aimed at covering the whole country. Marcos and myself are again invited as the lead presenters.

Current democratic governments and their senior civil servants must recognise rapidly that if they continue with their failing governance structures, history will judge them as being responsible for the increasing public disillusionment with the governing establishment and democracy itself. The great news is that some countries are now showing how the performance of the public sector can be dramatically improved, without risk. However, accusations of incompetence may soon be replaced by accusations of malicious neglect, with current management apparently deliberately ignoring improvements in other countries in order to protect themselves and the status quo, at the expense of the public, tax payers and even democracy. Populists will destroy the current political parties under such circumstances, but unfortunately could also hasten the move to autocracy of left or right, and a potential return to the wars of the 18th century.

However, I am optimistic that Brazil and Singapore will be catalysts for global change and that another UK "Sabrina" will rise and show the way! To be early followers of best practice isn't difficult, but needs self confidence and vision to reproduce and even enhance proven processes and release the energies and skills of all employees.

In order to overcome the weakness of the short term governance period of democracies, ideally all political parties should unite behind a policy of organisation reform of the State Sector, hence overcoming any attempts at blocking and delay until the next Government. The continuance of an effective democracy is far more important than short term party political advantage.

6 - SUMMARY

The prime purpose of this book has been to analyse the cause of democratisation peaking around the end of the 20th century and then starting to decline over the last 20 years. It is no coincidence that the conclusions relating to the failure of various aspects of Governance return to the same fundamental flaw across all democracies. The quality of Governance in Democracies, particularly in relation to Public Services, is recognised as the prime cause of public discontent, impacting quality of life, economic well being and sense of security, both personally and nationally. The common factor worldwide is the State Sector organisation structures, which are invariably focused on central control through functional, multi tiered bureaucracies, resulting in few having full responsibility, authority and accountability for delivering quality services. The only exceptions are Singapore, which decentralised their public sector some years ago and have had double the GDP growth of western democracies and good public satisfaction with their public services. If a counter argument is that it is a smaller country so not comparable, my response to that would be that it was when dynamic, smaller companies in the 80s started beating larger companies with customer focus, service, latest technology and price, that the large companies then started to decentralise, reduce management layers and become considerably more efficient and customer focused. ABB and my own company were classic examples. Our overhead costs had to replicate closely those of our smaller competitors, with our advantage being international best practice and technologies being spread rapidly across our activities through our CoEs. Currently Brazil are also using OKRs to progressively break through the bureaucratic constraints of their Public Sector, which is now being enthusiastically spread across the country following dramatic improvements in service and public satisfaction. With this continued success, it could ultimately result in political parties moving away from the political extremes, as public confidence in the "establishment" improves. This oscillation between extremes of left and right can ultimately cause instability and collapse of democracy.

As a consequence of devolving authority, responsibility and accountability in my Company, this enabled considerable improvement in performance and elimination of customer complaints and investigations into failures. This also had the effect of freeing up time for the strategic thinking of myself and my senior executive, rather than fire fighting on many local failures. The same applies to governance of the country. So much time is spent by Ministers responding to local failures, that the time available to properly evaluate strategic issues, from economic growth to actions to counter global threats and criminal cartels is inevitably reduced. Believe me, the scale of this change was a shock to myself. The quality of democratic governance will inevitably be transformed to the benefit of the public.

Most private companies have recognised that to harness the skills and higher education standards of all of its employees makes it a formidable company. Sharing of views and experiences, identifying best practices world wide and then deciding the best way to legally use these to achieve a Company's objectives can be fundamental to optimising success. Encouraging and enabling all levels to contribute to customer satisfaction and company performance was one of my most exciting and fulfilling experiences, something not featured in autocracies or bureaucracies. The same should apply in Government and State Sectors, rather than languishing in the 19th century organisation mentality, treating employees as though they are incapable of accepting responsibilities.

Concerning Health Care, defenders claim that the NHS has less "managers" than other countries. This may be so, but the authority, responsibility and accountability of the "local" manager is key to being able to deliver a package of total patient care that meets the patients needs. If you have a multitude of functions/agencies to coordinate, all with differing priorities from the functional management, plus 12+ layers from the Chief Executive to a nurse, for example, then endless communication and coordination meetings result and the scope for slip ups multiply. The time that I spent on meetings when I moved from a functional and multi tiered organisation to a decentralised one reduced by 80%. Instead of coordination issues and solving problems, the focus changed to monitoring the key metrics, encouraging continuous improvement initiatives and strategic developments such as growth and new innovations. Government Ministers and their Senior Executives would think that they had arrived in a "new world". Instead of 80% of time fighting internal failures, 80% could be devoted to addressing the extremely serious global issues such as security, trading, environmental and financial challenges. What or who is holding them back?

The prime advantage that democracies have over autocracies is the freedom given to its private sector to innovate in a competitive environment, although autocracies are now trying to find routes to copy and overcome these disadvantages. China in particular is not ashamed to ban the 'not invented here syndrome" and seeks every way possible, including the apparent bypassing of intellectual property laws, to replicate best practice/technologies. For democracies to allow this, coupled with their use of slave labour, is an incredible act of self harm which has undermined the economic performance of democracies and companies, whilst also increasing dependancy on an autocracy that has a declared expansionist strategy that will increasingly undermine NATO countries. Whatever the immediate trading advantages may have been, which the "short termism" of democracies tends to encourage, the longer term security exposure could be devastating. Clear identification of the priority long term security objectives of not being exposed to future threats from unstable and power obsessed autocrats should have prevented all democracies from being exposed to a potentially dangerous confrontation, at a time when the democracies themselves have become economically weaker, with discontent and populism growing.

However, 40-60% of the GDP in democracies is actually State expenditure, and if the state sector operates with a bureaucratic organisation structure that effectively constrains change, then the positive impact of democracy is being inhibited by up to 60% of its full potential. A top heavy dictatorial approach is ultimately a recipe for disaster, particularly in a dynamic and rapidly changing world. No matter how brilliant the leader, the dissipation of his ideas through a large functional bureaucracy will be like the fading bow wave of an ocean liner. Believe me, I have tried it.

Success Criteria

The fundamentals for any service provider or company are
1.   Customer focused Community/ Area Manager with full authority, responsibility, accountability, including financials, to meet the customers needs.
2.   Skilled workforce committed to providing those services/products.
3.   Ideally this Manager should have all necessary facilities and employees under his/her direct control, but in larger Companies and for non core activities, this may not be possible or even desirable.
4.   All "subcontracted" services/materials must be under the local managers control, by contract, with alternative sourcing options as necessary. This applies to both "internal' and "external" services/suppliers.

In the State Sector currently, only number 2 exists. In my experience, the greater the number of "sub suppliers", the greater the quality of management control is needed and risk of failure increases. However this can be mitigated by having either alternative sources of supply which can also result in more competitive prices, or longer term partnership agreements, which my company used to great effect.

The use of OKRs (Objectives and Key Results), particularly in a large organisation, is a structured approach to management and control of "internal suppliers", which ensures that management actions and decision making are constantly referenced back to the prime objectives and the intermediate key results necessary for success, as summarised in Appendix 1. Sometimes this may seem a little pedantic, but I have found that doing the simple things diligently and consistently well and in a structured way is fundamental to success, as is the KISS philosophy, "keep it simple stupid". Leading international companies such as ABB and Google use the same philosophy. When referring to all the failures of Governance contained in this book, they relate to a failure of attention to the fundamentals of good management, which, for the State Sector, should primarily be focussed around the following;

a) Questioning and fully understanding the needs of customers/public in terms of services, security and economy.
b) Setting clear objectives to meet those needs
c) Identifying key results and actions to achieve those objectives.
d) Adapting these objectives to meet a Governments election manifesto commitments and evolving strategic objectives and events.
e) Identifying and applying international best practice.

Hopefully, Governments and the State Sectors recognise the threat, even to democracy itself, that many are now facing. This is the type of crisis that private companies face when heading for decline and bankruptcy. Rapid corrective action is now vital.

The fantastic news is that there is a proven way out, without risk, which will transform the quality of governance in terms of public services, the economy and internal security, which will also then help to strengthen national security longer term. The longer the delay in taking corrective action, the more difficult will be the consequences of continuing decline.

If, unlike Brazil, the State Sector does not take the initiative itself to immediately tackle its serious failings, then I would suggest that those responsible for current failures must also accept the consequences. If Governments and/or senior Civil Servants cannot accept the successful processes and structures used by most private companies and now Brazil and Singapore, then a conference of proactive Civil Servants, with experienced "organisation" consultants as presenters, should be held to inspire a way forward, as happened in Brazil. The use of OKRs provides an excellent discipline and process to achieve rapid improvement with minimal disruption. It would rapidly overcome the disfunctionality that exists in the Health Service, Transport, Education, Housing strategies, Policing, Prisons, MOD, Immigration, HMRC, Defence, Judiciary, in fact all facets of Governance currently, including local Government.

Considering international security, avoidance of dependency on autocratic regimes both financially or militarily should be the number 1 objective. Would Germany and the EU have allowed themselves to be so vulnerable to energy dependency on Russia if they had rigorously followed the OKRs process, rather than apparently letting short term economic pressures and top down wishful thinking lead the way. Or would the West be so dependent on high tech equipment, rare metals and micro chips from China? Or would democracies have allowed themselves to be vulnerable to penal loan terms from China linked to key strategic locations, such as ports in the Mediterranean or even Caribbean Islands? With the EU contributing only 1% to NATO because it apparently cannot afford more, this indicates where it places security and NATO in its list of priorities, particularly as Junker and Macron have separately said that the EU should have its own defence capability. If this implies independence from NATO, then this is potentially disastrous for world democracies, particularly if the rise in disillusionment with democracy and extremism continues to grow across Europe.

If the EU also becomes a Federal State, it will be vital that the EU overcomes its excessive bureaucracies in both Brussels and the member Countries to avoid a potential economic and security disaster at the heart of a major current democracy, which could rapidly become autocratic. The reality is that the EU Commission in Brussels appears to have greater relevance in terms of policy and administration of the EU than the elected Parliament, which has a rotating 6 monthly President, which could be construed as a token democratic gesture to the member countries. Conjecture over this is not the purpose of this book, but the devolvement of power away from Brussels is unfortunately difficult to envisage and could ultimately bring about its downfall as a result of the current growth of populists/extremists.

People issues

When considering employee factors related to fundamental organisation change, bureaucratic structures are orientated to be controlled by the centre and by definition are resistant to change and hence orientated against being dynamic or innovative. In such structures, change means risk and the status quo has enormous lifetime benefits for those career Civil Servants, particularly to those at the higher levels of such impenetrable structures, where the complexity ensures that no one can be held accountable for failures. Avoidance of risk also ensures job and pension security for life in many countries, with pay levels of most being above that in the private sector. The senior Management across the Public Sectors earn considerably more than UK Government Ministers, including the Prime Minister, and also have a lifetime of experience in the "sector". Hence, they are well versed, not only in the technical details of the sector, but also how to manipulate a new minister who is dependant on their knowledge and could also be moved on within a year or two, particularly if "mistakes" are made. Elected politicians then find it very difficult to impose organisation changes onto "reluctant" Government Departments, particularly when told that change will fail "so you, Minister, will be held accountable". If the Minister applies pressure, then this could result in a formal complaint about bullying behaviour which could ruin a career, even if found innocent some months later. When considering these factors and the considerable adverse economic impact of not resolving current inefficiencies, exacerbated by the increasing belligerence of autocracies such as Russia, China, Iran and North Vietnam, then Governments must urgently take corrective action. In contrast to Russia, China seems to be adopting a longer term strategy of waiting for bureaucratic democracies to implode.

The State Sector senior managers must be made fully accountable for their performance. Fear of change can be a real challenge to the best of us, but these fears can be managed by allowing those who would not want to be involved to relocate if possible, or accept early retirement or voluntary redundancy. In practice, the transition went exceptionally smoothly in the 12 state sector acquisitions that my company made, with the overwhelming majority welcoming the changes and asking why management didn't do it earlier. Using the first transformation as a reference point, others, including senior management, quickly demanded to follow, fearing being left behind. Managers at all levels rapidly became committed and all staff became proud of their achievements. Exactly the same is happening in Brazil. Expensive independent investigations into failures became a thing of the past. Incidentally, I never experienced such enquiries in any of the private international companies that I worked for. Such a recourse would have been an admission of senior management incompetence. With a decentralised structure, responsibility for failure is clearly identified to the fully accountable "local" key manager. With structured support from Centres of Excellence, failure was avoided, early corrective action being the prime objective. A supportive culture to all staff, from top to bottom, was a powerful way to overcome fear and minimise failure.

With good consultancy support, the devolved management team will work together to create the key objectives and key results (OKRs) to make their "service" a success, whilst also ensuring compliance with the sector's strategic objectives. This "ownership" of those key metrics to ensure that the needs of the customers/patients are met, acknowledges that this local team know their customers/patients better than anyone else. An initial "customer" survey also gives focus and awareness.

Vulnerability of Democracies to new Autocrats

The reality is that the evolvement of democracies or successful privatisation of companies is no guarantee that the positive impact will continue for ever. They need careful nurturing, monitoring and focus on achieving the" key objectives". The core benefits resulting from privatisation of British Rail, resulting in public satisfaction with UK Railways being the second highest in Europe in 2000, behind Finland, have been dissipated as a result of most now being operated by the lower "performing" State Railways of various European countries. Possibly the worst of all options!

The use of clear OKRs, for example, including focus onto customer satisfaction and the core reasons and factors for the success in the 90s, would have avoided the award of contracts to these State Operators, which has resulted in the current decline in standards to those previously existing in Europe, or even worse. In essence, UK railways have effectively been renationalised, but under the control of Europe, with Railtrack having been brought under UK state ownership 20 years ago. Some would justify this by saying that contracts were awarded by strict application of EU rules. However, my response would be to ask how France, for example, avoids allowing UK train operators or manufacturers to have contracts in France, but they demand the right to tender in the UK. An effective way of destroying the excellent private companies who took initial control of the UK Rail Operations.

Monaco is fully aware of the unreliability of French trains when taking staff to work from French towns along the coast. They fought for some years to run their own train service on French Railways to ensure that staff could arrive at work on time. Those who don't believe such statements or believe that French Railways are wonderful have never had to rely on those trains. We always took a taxi to Nice airport rather than rely on the early train, which was often late or cancelled. Virgin Trains ran a good service from Manchester to London, vastly increasing the number of services and passenger numbers. Now the new Italian State Railway owners, Avanti, have reduced services back to that of 30 years ago, with shortage of staff now said to be a problem. I never think about going to London for a day out now. This decline reminds me of an incident about 5 years ago, when I was buying a ticket from Nice to Venice. I asked for the cheapest economy class fare. I then asked the 1st class fare. I was told "Oh, if you want a first class, then that is cheaper than the best economy at the moment"! I was stumped for words at the marketing and logic of this "offer".

Finally, when considering that the EU has been deliberately

undermining the UK economy since Brexit, the UK is now relying on EU countries to seek a resolution to the Rail strikes, with failure having consequences on further public discontent, with the emotional and illogical cries being "nationalise the railways", "rejoin the EU" or "elect an extremist Party". Lack of awareness of the reasons for the success of the privatised railways of the 90s, coupled with the lack of strategic thinking, has allowed poorer performing, state subsidised, foreign railways to undercut those very successful Private Train Operators of the 90s.

Sustainability

The recent academic studies show the harsh reality that democratisation has gone passed its peak and is now in reverse after reaching the point of inflexion. Without urgent action, it is possible that this reversal will soon escalate into an "avalanche" over the next 10-30 years. Burying the "head in the sand" and hoping that the new autocracies will become benevolent is not an option. Also, financial manipulations by the major institutions, or changing Governments, will not magically take away the fundamental cause of democratisation starting to decline. The public is rightly dissatisfied with the quality of governance generally, which includes public services, the sense of economic well being and sense of security internally and externally.

Financial manipulations of Company accounts in order to dress up inadequate performance is a sign of a Company in trouble. My instruction to my Finance Director was to focus firstly on Management Accountancy and identify key actions with managers to optimise our internal performance and customer experiences. Translating this to Government performance, growth, investment, trends of debt to GDP, trade balance, capital employed, exchange rates and unemployment rates are indicative of the health of an economy, but crucially, the efficiency and size of the Public Sector can make or break a country. It controls and influences the quality of Governance, the standard of security internally and internationally and crucially the economic performance of the country compared to competitor nations. Taking the actions detailed in this book, interest rate rises to attract support for the currency would then become unnecessary. The fundamentals of the economy would then be strong as a result of good governance and efficiency, a prime attraction for investors in both currencies and shares.

The vast majority of democracies are burdened by public sector bureaucracies that were necessary in the industrial revolution, when most of the country was poorly educated and change was slow. Such structures today are a recipe for disaster in private companies. Why should the Public Sector be any different? Those who have to deliver services to the public know the frustrations linked to coordinating multi functions who have their own agenda and priorities. The good news for democracies is that this is totally within their control and has already been easily overcome without fear or risk. When relating this to Government finances, with public spending at 40-60% of GDP, then not only the quality and responsiveness of the public sector will be improved, but 12 to 20% of GDP can be available to reduce a country's debts and/or increase the effectiveness of public services, assuming the common inefficiency factor of 30%. In money terms, this equates to £300 billion in the UK. Why must the public be put through economic stress and increasing taxes to fund a Public Sector which doesn't appear to recognise its failings, or does, but doesn't know how to solve it? I personally believe that the vast majority in the Public Sector are like mine and many other Companies and Countries and would grasp the opportunity to be released from the "chains of bureaucracy" and replace it with a sense of pride in performance, as I witnessed in my company and in Brazil.

Core Action

The role of Government must be to establish, from its senior civil servants, whether they recognise this need for structural change and if so, how they intend to implement it. As in Brazil, a conference of senior Civil Servants with presentations by experienced managers who have transformed the performance and focus of State Sector bureaucracies would be ideal. Volunteers who would like to take the lead, like Sabrina in Brazil, or myself in the UK, should then be asked to lead the way. Any who are not committed should be offered voluntary redundancy or retirement and replaced. Experienced Consultancy help will be needed to ensure that the change process will be structured effectively and rapidly. Within a year major improvements will be in evidence and others will be pushing for implementation, with "in house" successes providing models for others to follow, as in Brazil and my own and many other Companies detailed earlier. Appointment of Centres of Excellence for the various types of Government services ensures in house rapid reference points for people to seek help. Every year of delay in the UK is costing around £300 billion of cost saving or improved services and unnecessary economic misery for the public.

I believe that these structural problems in Public Sector Governance ideally should become a non political issue if the decline in democratisation is to be reversed. All Democracies need to take urgent action to stop the current slow decline becoming an avalanche. Breaking the bureaucratic "chains" around democracies has never been more urgent than now. The economic revitalisation of democracies will also be a major security step to deter the circling autocracies. The realisation of the efficiency and performance improvements, outlined earlier in this book, could dramatically reduce the debts in Western Democracies, transform the speed of recovery from their current serious economic problems, whilst also reducing economic exposure and vulnerability to aggressive autocrats and criminal gangs. The Civil Servants should be leading the way, like those in Brazil. In the UK, they are being paid three times the salary of ministers and should be made accountable for their success/failures. Those embracing the change should be lauded for their initiative, because the scale of importance of this will only be fully appreciate in future years, as the differential with those countries who resist will rapidly become clear.

Improving the quality of governance generally will not only save democracy but will also improve the quality of management related to public services, security, the environment and "saving the planet" from autocracies. The key issue will be which countries will be in the lead and which will be engulfed by public unrest, populism, extremism and loss of democracy, joining the 10 who are already down this path.

Our book "Breaking The Chains Of Bureaucracy" (Amazon) details how performance transformations have been achieved in many countries. The rapid and dramatic improvements must surely be acted on by the many declining and economically troubled democracies, particularly across Europe. For every day's delay in the UK, for example, the potential cost to tax payers is approaching £1 Billion Pounds in terms of tax reduction or improved public services.

Total replacement of bureaucratic Governance in Democracies should be targeted within 4 years, enabling economies to be strengthened and negotiating power with Autocracies to be increased, when a new understanding or "entente cordiale" will have a better chance of succeeding.

Bureaucracies are a handicap to Democracies, but essential in Autocracies, which rely on strict central control.

The clock is ticking and the alarm bells are already ringing.

ACKNOWLEDGEMENTS

I would like to thank Marcos Barros for his incredible fortitude and inspirational efforts over many years, being Founder of Oxford Business Masters and co founder of "Salt of the Earth Mission", a large charity working with the Government and using OKRs to look after a population of over half a million people in the Health, Education and Social Care Sector in Brazil. More recently, he is responsible for the largest implementation of OKRs in both the Public and Private Sectors in Brazil, improving their performance to the benefit of the public. Conferences have motivated senior managers in the public sector to embark on a drive to improve the quality of services that could give the inspiration and confidence for global economies to replicate similar actions around the world. The avoidance of the collapse of global democracies could depend on the success and spread of the Brazilian "revolution". Marcos has shared his OKR process in Appendix 1 and has clients that include AT&T, SKY TV, Microsoft, GSK-GlaxoSmithKline and Easynet.

I would also like to congratulate:

Sabrina Baes, the senior Public Sector Manager in Brazil, for having the confidence and vision to respond to the presentation by Marcos, asking for his help to successfully apply OKRs in her Sector. This is now resulting in the public benefitting across Brazil as other Public Sector Departments increasingly seek to also improve the quality of their services by use of OKRs.

Paulo Ishikawa, originally MPMS Head of Strategic Planning, whose support and involvement helped the spread of OKRs. He is now an OKR "evangelist" in the Brazilian Council of Public Ministries.

Bianca Costa, MPMS General Secretary, whose support and encouragement were essential for the project to succeed.

Ludimila Silva, MPMS DAEX coordinator, whose enthusiasm for the methodology was contagious. Her sector was one of the first to reach outstanding results in the organisation.

Paulo Cesar Zeni is the President of the Artificial Intelligence Innovation Committee and is the driver for the innovations now happening in the MPMS. His encouragement and support helped to make OKRs happen.

Alexandre Mango Benites de Lacerda, the Attorney General of Justice of the Prosecutor's Office, who has overseen the formation of such a dynamic team.

Finally, thanks to my staff from top to bottom, including the unions, for their support in transforming BREL and providing a model for others to follow. They have every right to be proud, and their story is now an inspiration in Brazil and hopefully in the UK in the future. After Privatisation, my senior team, below, became global Centres of Excellence in their particular specialisms and became market leaders as we expanded globally.

Adrian Dean, Alan Dungworth, John Morgan, Dave Mumford, Brian Spencer, John Williams, Mike Willmot. At various critical stages, valuable support was given by Mike Conway, Nick King, Andrew Norris and finally Peter Lowe, who I used as a trail blazer in one of the first self contained Business Units created pre privatisation, developing from scratch an electric locomotive new vehicle assembly line at Crewe, delivering all on time and within budget. This was good news for me, because the fact that I was Works Manager at the time and had total faith in him and the workforce to deliver was most likely in the face of some who were opposed to the concept of decentralisation! The visit of the Queen to see the first loco roll off the production line added to the pressure. I knew that we had no chance with the old functional organisation!

I hope that the efforts of all of the above will inspire others to do the same, saving Democracies for the benefit of future generations.

APPENDIX 1

AN OVERVIEW OF OKRS - OBJECTIVES AND KEY RESULTS - MARCOS BARROS

Andy Grove created OKRs while he was INTEL CEO in the 70s. INTEL had lost ground on microprocessor sales to Motorola and Sinclair. He created Operation Crush to recover market share. They communicated and executed the strategy using OKRs and were back as market leaders within 2 years.

Then Google adopted OKRs and, after publishing a video showing how they use them, thousands of companies have adopted the framework to bring focus and alignment to their most important goals. According to Larry Page, co-founder of Google, OKRs kept the entire team aligned and in sync, becoming an essential methodology to fulfil their mission. Twenty years later, OKRs are still Google's framework of choice to create, communicate and manage goals.

An MIT Sloan Management Review of 124 organisations published in 2018, concluded that only 28% of executives and middle managers responsible for executing strategy could list three of their company's strategic priorities. It is little wonder that execution levels are so low. Although OKRs can bring about many other benefits, they are primarily a way to communicate and execute strategy, with progress being measured in an effective way.

OKR is the acronym for Objectives and Key Results, the two components of the framework. A good implementation will produce OKRs that:

- Are short and simple
- Are few in numbers, so are easy to remember
- Clearly state what the Objective is
- Have Key Results with numeric indicators to remove any ambiguity
- Have constraints and the measurable criteria for success

When creating OKRs, we usually do it in 2 levels. In level 1, the Senior Leadership Team translates the organisation's strategic priorities into 3 to 5 OKRs for the year.

Then, the Senior Leadership Team will select members of different departments and functions to build the second level of OKRs. They will cover only the first quarter of the year and will identify how they advance the level 1 organisation-wide ones.

Level 2 OKRs are the bridge between strategy and execution, creating short term goals. OKRs should be visible to the whole organisation, fostering transparency, accountability and alignment of efforts.

Once these two layers are established, the Management by OKRs is activated, with 20 minute weekly check-in meetings reviewing the 3Ps - Progress, Problems and Plans for the next 7 days. This also creates a mindset of continuous improvement.

The focus of the OKR approach provides an all embracing analysis to identify how to rapidly optimise, for example, patient care in the community. My team and I have developed this for a Health Care Service for 0.5 million people in Brazil, which has been very successful over many years and is funded by the State. It brings functional activities together under a "community' manager who will have full responsibility, authority and accountability. It also highlights deficiencies and corrective action as necessary, rather than some remote negotiations between ill informed senior Civil Servants and Ministers. The front end services leap with joy at such an approach, as did everyone involved in Brazil, many Companies and vast numbers in the private sector who now take this for granted. What isn't needed is a top down arbitrary head count chop of staff, which will only cause resentment and will not address the fundamental problems at the "front end", resulting in no commitment to make it work.

This is a brief overview of how OKRs are used to rapidly improve the performance of bureaucratic organisations. Greater details are contained in our book *Breaking The Chains Of Bureaucracy* (Amazon).

Showing it graphically:

BENEFITS

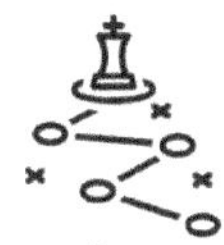

Strategic priorities are communicated in a simple and short format at all levels and strategy is executed.

Weekly focus on strategic priorities.

Alignment of efforts - everyone pulling towards the chosen priorities.

Better engagement through decentralisation of the planning process, bottom-up planning and weekly check-ins.

Move from task-completion mindset to results-oriented culture.